Praise for YEScarolina

"Jimmy Bailey's realization that the thrill, excitement and power of entrepreneurship can change young peoples' lives has in fact made that happen in our community and communities throughout South Carolina. For many of our young people, lessons learned about entrepreneurship can be one of the most important educational experiences of their lives. This book is proof of that."

Joseph P. Riley, Jr., Mayor
City of Charleston, South Carolina

"YEScarolina perfectly embodies the notion that entrepreneurial education is paramount to solving the problem of poverty. By nurturing the natural talents and attitudes of low income youth, YEScarolina gives kids the tools to transform street smarts into business smarts."

Steve Mariotti, Founder
Network for Teaching Entrepreneurship

"Jimmy Bailey's passion for YEScarolina is palpable—in person and in print. YEScarolina is not only a great South Carolina story, but a heartwarming, American story."

Walter Edgar, Radio Host
"Walter Edgar's Journal" on ETV-SC

"These kids have mastered the critical skill of turning challenges into opportunities, which is just as valuable off the court as it is on."

Pat Williams, Senior VP
NBA's Orlando Magic

"For teachers everywhere who have asked themselves 'What is it all for?' here is the answer. These stories are a reminder that we CAN make a difference in the lives of our students. YEScarolina plants the seeds of youth entrepreneurship into the fertile minds of students across South Carolina."

Paul Smith Jr. MBA, Assistant Professor of Business
Newberry College

"A wonderful tribute to the memory of Mark Motley. These stories are an inspiration for educational professionals everywhere."

Aimee R. Gray, Certified Entrepreneurship Teacher

TEACHERS
REACHING
OUT

TEACHERS
REACHING
OUT

25 *DEDICATED SOULS who have changed the lives of young entrepreneurs from YEScarolina and the Mark Elliott Motley Foundation*

Published by Advantage, Charleston, South Carolina.
Member of Advantage Media Group.

ADVANTAGE is a registered trademark and the Advantage colophon is a trademark of Advantage Media Group, Inc.

Printed in the United States of America.

ISBN: 978-1-59932-262-9
LCCN: 2011940638

This publication is designed to provide accurate and authoritative information in regard to the subject matter covered. It is sold with the understanding that the publisher is not engaged in rendering legal, accounting, or other professional services. If legal advice or other expert assistance is required, the services of a competent professional person should be sought.

Advantage Media Group is proud to be a part of the Tree Neutral® program. Tree Neutral offsets the number of trees consumed in the production and printing of this book by taking proactive steps such as planting trees in direct proportion to the number of trees used to print books. To learn more about Tree Neutral, please visit www.treeneutral.com. To learn more about Advantage's commitment to being a responsible steward of the environment, please visit www.advantagefamily.com/green

TreeNeutral

Advantage Media Group is a leading publisher of business, motivation, and self-help authors. Do you have a manuscript or book idea that you would like to have considered for publication? Please visit www.amgbook.com or call 1.866.775.1696

In loving memory of

Mark Elliott Motley

JULY 15, 1972 – FEBRUARY 13, 2000

My son Mark was a young man of extraordinary courage. At the age of 27, he was dedicated to the mission of self-betterment through a painful medical procedure, one to hopefully better control his epilepsy. I realized what a remarkable man he had become when he tackled his epilepsy so strongly and bravely, though it ultimately cost him his life. I felt such love and pride in him, and deep awe at the courage he displayed. Mark was gentle but strong, kind, generous. He was deeply loyal and always the first to forgive. He kept our family focused on the simple but important things in life and he led our family through many happy times and through rough waters in his very quiet, unassuming way. He so loved his family, his friends, the sea – enjoying the water and the sky – and the music of Jimmy Buffet. His courage and strength are a tribute to us all and he is never far from my mind nor from my heart.

– RONALD L. MOTLEY

FOREWORD

"Solving the Problem of Poverty"

*Excerpt from speech at a Hillsdale College seminar
held in Memphis, Tennessee, May 1998*

*"I know a secret which, if fully understood by our government,
business, and community leaders, could have enormous positive
implications for the future of our society. Simply put, the secret
is this: Children born into poverty have special gifts that prepare
them for business formation and wealth creation. They are
mentally strong, resilient and full of chutzpah. They are skeptical
of hierarchies and the status quo. They are long suffering in the
face of adversity. They are comfortable with risk and uncertainty.
They know how to deal with stress and conflict.*

*"These are the attitudes and abilities that make them ideally
suited for breaking out of the cycle of dependency that so often
comes with poverty and for getting ahead in the marketplace.
In short, poor kids are 'street smart,' or what we at the National
Foundation for Teaching Entrepreneurship [name since changed
to Network for Teaching Entrepreneurship] call 'business smart.'
Precisely because of their poverty — that is, because of their
experience surviving in a challenging world — they are able to
perceive and pursue fleeting opportunities that others, more
content with their lot in life, tend to miss."*

STEVE MARIOTTI
President and founder
Network for Teaching Entrepreneurship

That was the speech that changed my life. It spoke to me, it reminded me of myself, and it brought me to where I am today. For five years, I couldn't stop thinking about that speech. I wanted to act on it, but didn't know how. Eventually, I enrolled in a NFTE teacher training session and was on my way to starting YEScarolina. Seven years later, YEScarolina through NFTE University had trained over 500 teachers and touched the lives of thousands of kids in South Carolina. Steve Mariotti helped change the way we look at education, and the teachers you will find featured in this book are carrying out this mission day in and out.

We have featured their students in our book series "The Spirit of Outreach," and now it's time to recognize the teachers behind these amazing students. They have a gift for bringing the real world into the classroom and engaging their students in a whole new way. They are the kind of teachers who inspire you, the kind with the ability to change your life, and the kind you always remember. YEScarolina is the organization providing our educators with the necessary tools, but these teachers are the real heroes.

James J. Bailey, founder, president and executive director of YEScarolina, has witnessed a recurring theme in life: people can achieve great success if they are given the tools and the chance. In addition to his work with YEScarolina, Jimmy served three terms in the South Carolina State House of Representatives. He is also president of Bailey and Associates, a commercial real estate firm. He is also an active supporter of the Network for Teaching Entrepreneurship (NFTE) in South Carolina, reflecting his belief that entrepreneurship can connect young people to the community and the workplace.

TEACHERS WITH THE SPIRIT OF OUTREACH

Lancie Affonso

College of Charleston

Collegiate level; youth 9-12 grades

"I foster competition and innovation and constantly challenge the students to do better."

Communication matters most says Lancie Affonso, who rallies 16 years of teaching experience to work with young entrepreneurs striving to turn their passions into profits. His students learn to build skills in networking, presentations, and sales pitches. Affonso lives in Charleston and is an adjunct professor of Computer Science as well as Management and Entrepreneurship at the College of Charleston.

Why I teach

The reason I teach is because I want to make a difference. I am passionate about learning new technologies and business processes. Teaching affords me the opportunity to be a lifelong learner and share what I learn with my students. I realize the importance of my job and feel blessed that I love what I do on a daily basis. I teach and learn at the same time. How lucky am I?

What my kids learn about innovation and entrepreneurship

My students learn how to be next-generation entrepreneurs by leveraging technology and by building on their entrepreneurial skills. For example, students conduct market research and learn about innovative ways to reach their target market including the design and creation of mobile iPhone and Android apps for their businesses.

How I teach them to be motivated to succeed

I want my students to be excited about what they do to earn a living and to fulfill their dream of starting a business. We use digital storytelling techniques and multimedia (YouTube, etc.) to help them explore show them the thriving businesses that some of the students in the YEScarolina entrepreneurship program have started. We encourage our students to take calculated risks and to take charge of their destiny. "Twenty years from now you will be more disappointed by the things that you didn't do than by the ones you did do. So throw off the bowlines. Sail away from the safe harbor. Catch the trade winds in your sails. Explore. Dream. Discover."–*Mark Twain*

My secret approach to unleashing students' creativity

I foster competition and innovation and constantly challenge the students to do better.

What I do to teach self-confidence

During these times in society, teaching self-confidence to kids has probably become more important than ever before because of the exposure and ease at which external factors can influence us nowadays with the advent of the Internet and cell phones. Students do "elevator" pitches with sponsors/investors [brief summaries that would be possible to deliver during an elevator ride].

My students' most important leadership skills

The ability to communicate effectively and lead by example. My students understand that one of the best ways to lead is by example – pitching in where needed, lending a helping hand, and making sure that the work you do is clearly understood by your entrepreneurship team.

The best way for them to learn those skills

Presentations, networking, starting their own businesses, and convincing investors and customers about the merits of their ideas.

The most important thing teaching has taught me

To be the student – it changes my perspective.

How has YEScarolina helped you develop your ability to teach entrepreneurial skills?

The fastest way for South Carolina to grow more jobs is to attract, nurture and help small firms launched by ambitious entrepreneurs. YEScarolina has helped me reach out to these future entrepreneurs by providing free high impact entrepreneurship workshops and networking opportunities with teachers across the state.

Any special stories you'd like to share?

I teach undergraduate and MBA courses, and my entrepreneurship students are often amazed when we watch the YouTube video of one of the YEScarolina "Rose Kids," Damian Brown, with his Palmetto Rose business [selling rose-shaped decorations made from palmetto fronds]. Damian was one of my students from Sanders-Clyde School and the YEScarolina Advanced Entrepreneurship Program, and the return on investment in his rose business is more than many of what my college students can hope to achieve with their business plans.

Linda Avery

Crescent High School, Sumter

9th-12th grades

"Not only should they think 'outside the box,' they should build a new box."

"**E**nthusiasm and perseverance are the traits that will turn a young person with creative ideas into a future business leader," says Linda Avery. She brings seven years of teaching experience to what she sees as a "divine appointment." Avery lives in Sumter.

Why I teach

I teach because I believe that I've been given a divine appointment! Teaching was absolutely not on my radar as a young person, but I am grateful to have been afforded the opportunity to have a positive impact on the life of some young person through my words, guidance and instruction.

What my kids learn about innovation and entrepreneurship

My students learn that, to be involved in business, one must learn to think creatively; not only should they think "outside the box," they should build a new box. They learn to look at old and familiar things in a totally new way. They also learn that the most successful entrepreneurs are those who reach back to help others achieve.

How I teach them to be motivated to succeed

When an individual student, a duo, or a group is presenting ideas, projects or assignments to the class, I frequently say: "Remember, no hating, and no self-hating, either! You're the best, so tell us why you're the best!"

My secret approach to unleashing students' creativity

Individual attention, coupled with a sincerely caring attitude and a sense of humor.

What I do to teach self-confidence

Instead of telling a student that what he did was wrong, I ask him how he can improve on what he has – how could he make it better? Then I make sure to praise the attempt.

My students' most important leadership skills

The bravery it takes to stand in front of one's peers and talk about one's ideas; the perseverance to carry an idea out to fruition; and the enthusiasm to want to tell as many people as possible about the idea.

The best way for them to learn those skills

The best way is through taking the entrepreneurship class (of course!) and stepping up to compete in the business plan competition.

The most important thing teaching has taught me

What is right for one is not necessarily right for all. I have taught several semesters of entrepreneurship, and I have had to make adaptations and adjustments each time I teach it. What I have to offer must be the best fit for the students who are there at that present time.

Norma Brown

Dutch Fork High School, Irmo

10th-12th grades

"Students have so many God-given talents inside of them, and it is my job to show them how to release those talents."

Each of Norma Brown's students is as special as the next. She makes sure they all know that – and that caring about people more than money is what ultimately will bring them the greatest success. Brown lives in Irmo and has 28 years of teaching experience.

Why I teach

This is where God wants me to be, and I love to see young people grow and achieve in every aspect of life. I know that all students can learn, and I love to see them reach their potential in everything that they do.

What my kids learn about innovation and entrepreneurship

My students learn not only how to start a business but how to believe in themselves and their God-given talents. They learn how to think for themselves and how to take an idea and make it work and how to communicate the information that they have learned to others.

How I teach them to be motivated to succeed

I teach students individually. I show them that they are just as special as anyone else and how to care about people more than money. I teach to their interests, and I show them how they can use the information I teach them in a real-life experience. I give them the foundation, and I love to watch what they add and watch them grow and come alive in what they have learned.

My secret approach to unleashing students' creativity

I make them believe in themselves and know that if they set goals, use strategies to reach those goals, and interact with positive and successful people, the sky's the limit for them! I love to have guest speakers – ones who have had some of the same experiences they have and are now successful – speak to the students and encourage them. I show them I care about them, and about what affects them, by actions and words so when I do have to correct them they know I am correcting them out of love and concern.

What I do to teach self-confidence

First I make them list all of the positive things about themselves. Then I ask them to tell me about their dreams and goals, and then I show them what they can do to reach their goals. I try to be a role model by telling some hard experiences I had in my life and how God and hard work helped me through those times. I teach them not to be afraid of going through an open door and taking opportunities – because their ultimate blessing could be behind that door.

My students' most important leadership skills

I think their most important leadership skills are the ability to take the initiative and follow through on what they start, to believe in what they are doing, and to use their skills to encourage others. You have to believe in yourself and surround yourself with good people. Leaders are only as good as the people who follow them or surround them.

The best way for them to learn those skills

First I demonstrate the skill, or a peer demonstrates it; then, they do it by themselves. I give them instructions, and when they make mistakes they tell me what they should have done differently and what they could do differently next time.

The most important thing teaching has taught me

All students can learn. Students have so many God-given talents inside of them, and it is my job to show them how to release those talents and use them to help themselves and to help others. They don't care how much you know until they know how much you care! When they know you care about them personally, the sky is the limit as to what they can achieve.

How has YEScarolina helped you develop your ability to teach entrepreneurial skills?

YEScarolina has helped me in so many ways. I have been teaching entrepreneurship for over 20 years, and taking this class has given me a new perspective on teaching the course. I have learned so many techniques and different strategies. The book is awesome, and I would love to have it in my classroom. I have also learned so much from my students about technology. I also learned how important it is to bring in people from the community to connect with the students.

Any special stories you'd like to share?

I love the way we could use technology to teach students about business plans. It was great to see the students teach others all of the things they learned. Best of all were the end-of-the-course presentations. The students felt good about having professionals judge their presentations and giving them advice. The girl who won at my site was having a hard time with family but in spite of that did an awesome job in class – and therefore got an opportunity to display her business at the mall and talk about it to other young people.

Any additional comments?

Every child should be able to take an entrepreneurship class. I have seen how it can transform children into new and exciting people who believe in themselves and can achieve anything.

Tracy Cook

R.D. Anderson Applied Technology Center, Moore
10th-12th grades

"No matter how difficult my day has been, someone else has had a worse day, so I make it my daily goal to be the sunshine in all of my students' day."

A teacher needs to build self-confidence by offering praise and encouragement: That's the philosophy of Tracy Cook, who has been doing so for 19 years and instills that trait in students, asking them to write anonymous notes of praise to one another. Cook lives in Inman.

Why I teach

I find it rewarding and I love what the job involves: working with adolescents, inspiring youth, shaping and molding minds, and sharing knowledge to help youth grow daily.

What my kids learn about innovation and entrepreneurship

My students learn that in an ever-changing world, they will continuously be introduced to something new. As future entrepreneurs, their goal should be to always be a thinker and observer and to look for ways to improve what is already invented and/or to use their creativity to come up with a new idea that could turn into a promising opportunity.

How I teach them to be motivated to succeed

I talk to my students about their goals and creating a reasonable timeline for accomplishing them. We talk about how a positive attitude, determination, and dedication will help them be successful.

My secret approach to unleashing students' creativity

I introduce them to new inventions and businesses through videos and articles. I also allow them to create/invent using materials and equipment I supply and then hold a competition to see who has the most creative invention.

What I do to teach self-confidence

I praise them for work well done, reward them for certain accomplishments, and compliment them on their appearance. Periodically, I have students write one positive comment about another student on an index card and turn it into me without their name on it. Then the next day I give it to the student it was meant for.

My students' most important leadership skills

Teamwork: When in small groups, they work well together by sharing the workload and communicating effectively.

The best way for them to learn those skills

I help students learn leadership skills through modeling and reinforcing what is expected of them as team players.

The most important thing teaching has taught me

No matter how difficult my day has been, someone else has had a worse day, so I make it my daily goal to be the sunshine in all of my students' day.

How has YEScarolina helped you develop your ability to teach entrepreneurial skills?

I have learned to be a better negotiator in situations that require it, and I am continuously brainstorming invention and business ideas.

Frances G. Daniels

Florence Career Center, Florence
10th-12th grades

"By believing in yourself, you develop strength and become confident."

A first step on the path to entrepreneurial success," says Frances G. Daniels, "is for students to learn that they have creative potential waiting to be tapped. Anyone who wants to own a business can do so." Daniels, who has been teaching for seven years, lives in Florence.

Why I teach

I love to inspire students to do what they need to do to achieve their goals.

What my kids learn about innovation and entrepreneurship

My kids learn that they are creative. They learn that no idea is stupid. Therefore, they learn how to act and produce whatever they want. By doing this, students can become entrepreneurs. Each student is taught he or she could own a business.

How I teach them to be motivated to succeed

I teach my students to be motivated to succeed by being a motivator myself. Knowing and understanding the definition of "motivated" helps them to be creative when asked to proceed on a project.

My secret approach to unleashing students' creativity

My secret approach is to inform the students there are no boundaries when it comes to creativity.

What I do to teach self-confidence

I teach the students that they must believe in themselves. By believing in yourself, you develop strength and become confident.

My students' most important leadership skills

Teamwork, confidence, and attitude.

The best way for them to learn those skills

As a teacher, I model leadership skills. After modeling them, I have the students practice them among their peers.

The most important thing teaching has taught me

Wherever you are isn't necessarily where you will stay. With innovation, students can learn and adapt to any situation.

How has YEScarolina helped you develop your ability to teach entrepreneurial skills?

YEScarolina has helped me to know the subject well and have patience with the students as they adapt to the different learning skills.

Any special stories you'd like to share?

The excitement of students as they build upon their entrepreneurial skills was a very rewarding experience for me as the teacher. Students used the gaming technique to reinforce and enhance their own skills as well as to teach their peers.

Any additional comments?

YEScarolina has opened the minds of many students in the past couple of years. Students look forward to taking my entrepreneurship classes. My classes are usually full. Being able to explain their business plans in their presentations and using PowerPoint has enhanced my students' confidence and attitudes as they appear before entrepreneurial judges. This in itself builds great leaders with determination.

Melissa Ann Epps
Lakewood High School, Sumter
9th-12th grades

"Students are astonished that they can create a business from their hobby."

Once students develop confidence in themselves, says Melissa Ann Epps, "they are able to soar high as the sky." When she senses uncertainty, she addresses it so that every young person feels empowered to pursue a passion. Epps lives in Shiloh, Sumter County, and has taught for eight years at Lakewood High.

Why I teach

In 2003, I decided it was time for a career change. I decided to teach high school students, because I want to inspire the lives of teens through education. Every child deserves the right to be aware of educational opportunities.

What my kids learn about innovation and entrepreneurship

Students learn they can become successful by creating a business that is a passion to them. Students are astonished that they can create a business from their hobby. Students also learn that you have to continue to invest in your business to reach the maximum growth opportunity.

How I teach them to be motivated to succeed

I motivate students my sharing past YEScarolina success stories and the story of Dr. Farrah Gray [who rose from poverty to become a self-made millionaire at age 14]. They are surprised to learn that young people can start a business and become a millionaire at an early age.

My secret approach to unleashing students' creativity

Students' creativity is unleashed when I allow them to work as a team to develop a product, research the need, determine the cost, set the price for the product, and project how much money they can make in one year.

What I do to teach self-confidence

I teach them to support their response whether right or wrong because good businesspeople can convince a customer that their product/service is best. Students are required to stand and introduce themselves to the class and present projects throughout the course. When students are uncertain about things, their self-confidence is low, so I teach students beyond curriculum standards. Once they have gained self-confidence, they are able to soar high as the sky.

My students' most important leadership skills

Students' most important leadership skills involve the ability to organize and delegate tasks as a leader. Soft skills are also important as a leader. The leader must be able to communicate, show good work ethics, and work well with others.

The best way for them to learn those skills

Students learn best by doing and learning from their peers. Leaderships skills are taught through role play and scenarios that must be presented to the class and recorded on video. The students then critique themselves on how well they performed and what needs to be done to improve their performance.

The most important thing teaching has taught me

If you open a doorway for students and encourage them to walk through, all things are possible for both the student and teacher. I've learned that students have innovative minds; it is a matter of showing them how to communicate their creativity to others.

How has YEScarolina helped you develop your ability to teach entrepreneurial skills?

With training and supplemental resources through YEScarolina, I'm able to use content that is on the individual student's academic level and provide growth opportunity. The additional lessons allow innovation. YEScarolina is an awesome organization that allows students to improve their economic situation through starting and owning a small business.

Aimee R. Gray

Crescent High School, Iva

9th-12th grades

"The key here is to convince students that it's not about the money, but more about turning their passions and interests into a career that, if managed correctly, can be financially rewarding."

Aimee R. Gray lends each of her students $20 as start-up capital and proudly watches them learn that it's not just "other people" who start businesses. She saw two girls make $1,800 in three months and start planning for college. A teacher for seven years, she lives in Anderson.

Why I teach

I want to make a difference that will outlive me.

What my kids learn about innovation and entrepreneurship

After leaving my class, my kids can no longer encounter a problem without assessing it as a potential opportunity. I teach kids to take action to impact their communities and themselves in a profitable way.

How I teach them to be motivated to succeed

It's hard to teach motivation. Most kids are motivated by money – in this case, entrepreneurship is an easy sell. The key here is to convince students that it's not about the money, but more about turning their passions and interests into a career that, if managed correctly, can be financially rewarding. If they can't pinpoint what they're good at and like doing, they fall into the trap of trying to make money for money's sake – and when the hard work comes, they bail because it's not enjoyable.

My secret approach to unleashing students' creativity

Practice, practice, practice. The more creative thinking we do, the better the kids become at it. For some, it takes a while to chip away at all of the "stuff" layered on top of their creativity.

What I do to teach self-confidence

I treat each class as a family. Families build each other up and support each other. Fear of public speaking, trying new things, and failing miserably does not exist when we're all in it together. My students present to their classmates weekly, and they never stand up without first introducing themselves. The more times they do it, the easier it becomes and they become confident enough to present themselves to others outside of class.

My students' most important leadership skills

The ones they naturally possess. It's important to understand strengths and how to best use them. Trying to stuff a square peg in a round hole never works.

The best way for them to learn those skills

The best way for them to learn those skills is to practice them. They have to realize what their skills are as a leader and perfect those, and then surround themselves with people who possess skills that they lack. I also think it's valuable to show students examples of good and bad leadership styles. Simple things like watching the television show "The Apprentice," and having them write an explanation of where they think the project manager did well or failed, helps them analyze their own actions as a leader.

The most important thing teaching has taught me

Teaching has taught me open-mindedness and how to prioritize what students really need to know. Kids are so smart in very different ways, and teaching has helped me appreciate that it takes everyone to make the world go around. If a kid hates school but is passionate about playing the guitar, it's my job to help that child figure out how school can help him become a more successful musician. I want every student to be able to follow his or her dream – and make money in the process!

How has YEScarolina helped you develop your ability to teach entrepreneurial skills?

YEScarolina has helped me in so many ways. The YEScarolina teacher training that I took as a first-year teacher opened my eyes to a new way of educating. The fun, action-packed lessons changed the way I teach. I figured out along the way that students may be masters of memorization for a test, but unless they want to learn, they won't. I have thought about people like Andrew Jackson and Richard Branson who didn't become successful because of what they learned in school, but took it upon themselves to study their passions. And about one of the foremost ornithologists in the world who credits his second-grade teacher (who took his class outside every day to study birds) for his success. These people became inspired to want to know more and then found a way to make it happen. YEScarolina has helped me realize that if I can inspire my students to want to become entrepreneurs, teaching them how will be a breeze.

Any special stories you'd like to share

My favorite moment in teaching entrepreneurship is always at the beginning of the school year or biz camp when I tell the students that they will start a business during our time together. A light shines inside them when they realize it's not just "other people" who can be entrepreneurs. I lend each of my students $20 to start a small business. In some cases, they can only buy one item to sell, but it's fun to see them re-invest their earnings and, in many cases, build a viable business. One pair of students combined their start-up capital to start a personalized drawstring bag business. They started selling to friends, and as word spread their orders started to pour in. They began to come up with ways to expand their business such as creating fund-raisers for the school athletic teams, and branching out to travel softball teams. They took orders via e-mail and set up a supply chain. It was very gratifying to see their business organically grow and their enthusiasm soar as they saw increased profits. Within three months, the two girls had a net profit of over $1,800, and they decided to continue their education in college with entrepreneurship in mind.

Laura H. Gasque

Latta High School, Latta

9th-12th grades

"If people aren't willing to put in the hard work and take a risk on their ideas, then society could become stagnant. Entrepreneurs bring about innovation in society."

The simplest ideas, says Laura H. Gasque, are often best. Students can start small and by dreaming big can attain marvelous results. Each student, she knows, has a gift, whether it's recognized or not. Gasque lives in Floyd Dale Community in Dillon County. She has been teaching for 14 years.

Why I teach

My reasons are selfish. I believe that by educating children, I am doing my part in making the world a better place. I want to make a positive difference in the world.

What my kids learn about innovation and entrepreneurship

They learn that the world is constantly changing, and this change brings about an opportunity for new ideas. Every successful business started out as someone's idea. Some people may have thought the idea was zany at the time, but through perseverance and a belief in himself, the entrepreneur made it happen. Success also requires hard work, and if people aren't willing to put in the hard work and take a risk on their ideas, then society could become stagnant. Entrepreneurs bring about innovation in society.

How I teach them to be motivated to succeed

No matter how old a student is, he/she is still a child, and all children want to feel loved and accepted. I let them know that I care about them and that I believe in them. I take an interest in their business plans and their ideas and continuously try to encourage them to take them one step further. If they know I care about them, they will want to make me happy in return and will work harder for me in class.

My secret approach to unleashing students' creativity

We do some "artsy" projects in here as well as textbook-related projects. These creativity projects have very few guidelines, and my students are allowed to think outside the box. I have also found that laughter makes my students more comfortable in the classroom so they feel more at ease with introducing nontraditional things to their fellow classmates.

What I do to teach self-confidence

I never tell students that their ideas aren't any good, and I always try to emphasize the best parts of an idea. If I have a student who is more introverted than the others, I make it a point to call attention to something that student has done particularly well, even if it was not the most spectacular idea in the room.

My students' most important leadership skills

I believe that, in order to be good leaders, students need to focus on three areas. 1) They should have good communication skills so that their team members know what is expected of them. 2) They need to have good teamwork skills because they should know how to work with a group without being overbearing or dismissive to the team, and they need to be able to determine what each team member can bring to the group and utilize those qualities. 3) They need to learn responsibility and that they either win as a team or lose as a team, but blame should not be put on one person.

The best way for them to learn those skills

To work in groups toward a common goal, giving each student a chance to manage the group.

The most important thing teaching has taught me

All students are different, and each of them has a gift. Sometimes these gifts are obvious, but sometimes you have to do something to make the students themselves see their merits.

How has YEScarolina helped you develop your ability to teach entrepreneurial skills?

In 2006, I took the NFTE Training Workshop at Francis Marion University because I wanted to pursue new courses that I could teach at my high school. Sam Bryant was the teacher who conducted much of the training, and his excitement in the whole program was truly inspiring. He shared a lot of good ideas that I still use. I had not planned to take the graduate class that followed, but I found the workshop so helpful and enlightening that I immediately signed up and was further inspired by Dr. Joe Aniello. Their enthusiasm helped me to see the importance of entrepreneurship in society as well as the importance of young people finding their path for the future. YEScarolina has also helped me obtain supplies to teach my class. Because of them, I have a classroom set of textbooks. Jimmy Bailey and his staff have always been there to answer any questions that I have, and the newsletters and e-mails that I receive from them have given me lots of new materials to share with my students. It would have been much harder for me to teach this class if I had not had YEScarolina to help me.

Any special stories you'd like to share?

I have learned that the simplest ideas are usually the best. My favorite business plans are the ones where the students start small and dream big.

Any additional comments?

I began teaching through the Critical Needs Program in 1998. With a background in accounting, I worked in the business world before entering the classroom. I see the importance of small business and new business in society, and I think that entrepreneurship is one of the most important classes any student interested in business can take. It gives students a taste of all different aspects of business that they would cover if they pursued a business degree. It encourages them to envision their place in society. I also love the fact that it focuses on social responsibility as well.

Tonya Hanser

Lake City High School, Lake City

9th-12th grades

"You have to be a good follower before you can be a good leader."

Each student is unique, says Tonya Hanser, and each is motivated differently. She asks students to aim high for achievable goals. Their competitive instincts, she has learned, help to foster creativity as they learn to work together in groups. Hanser lives in Florence and has been teaching for six years.

Why I teach

I teach because I love learning, love knowledge, love ideas, and love my content area. Every day is different and unpredictable, which makes my job fascinating.

What my kids learn about innovation and entrepreneurship

Don't be afraid to take an idea and turn it into something profitable. If it doesn't work the first time, try again, and again, and again.

How I teach them to be motivated to succeed

For me, this is the hardest part of teaching because each student is different and requires a different motivation. What works for one student may or may not work for the rest of the class. In order to motivate students to succeed, I use different teaching methods, set high but achievable expectations, and place a value on learning by providing them with specific reasons for learning something.

My secret approach to unleashing students' creativity

Young people, by their nature, are a pretty creative bunch. When I add the element of competition and working in small groups, some of them respond by kicking that creativity up a notch. The result of that extra energy and creativity can be seen adorning the walls in my classroom and viewed on my teacher webpage.

What I do to teach self-confidence

The most important self-confidence strategy is providing leadership opportunities for students. Cultivating important characteristics, including responsibility and independence, by assigning students to different classroom and group roles can help build confidence and erase fear of trying new experiences. Reassuring students that they are capable of greatness and providing them with encouragement shows them my commitment to their success.

My students' most important leadership skills

You have to be a good follower before you can be a good leader.

The best way for them to learn those skills

Practice being a good follower at school and home; and of course, I, as the teacher, have to play an important role by setting an example.

The most important thing teaching has taught me

Patience and flexibility.

How has YEScarolina helped you develop your ability to teach entrepreneurial skills?

As a result of my NFTE training through YEScarolina, I am definitely more confident in teaching entrepreneurship. The activities that accompany the NFTE curriculum provide creative ways of introducing entrepreneurship and business concepts. The week training that I received from YEScarolina was the pivotal point in my decision to want to teach entrepreneurship. The instructors carried the class step by step through the activities and the process of creating our own business plan. Applying those same skills in my own classroom has created an interactive learning environment that benefits both me and my students. Also, I am now teaching summer camps and spreading the entrepreneurial spirit to younger students in my district.

Any additional comments?

I am very grateful to be a part of the NFTE and YEScarolina organizations. Their efforts in making sure teachers have the necessary tools to effectively teach entrepreneurship have made such an impact in my teaching.

Michele Jackson

Berea High School, Greenville

9th-12th grades, self-contained classes

"Many of my students have to survive due to their home life. They are motivated, headstrong and driven. "

"What makes you happy?" That's the question that Michelle Jackson asks her students, over and over again, until they finally share their dreams – and learn they can develop them into a profitable career. Jackson's own passion is teaching – particularly, life skills for a tough world – and she has been at it for eight years. She lives in Greenville.

Why I teach

I decided to become a teacher after 11 years of working with adolescents who had drug, alcohol and mental-health issues. I felt that I could better serve their needs in the classroom as a special-education teacher. Teaching gives me the opportunity to provide my students with life skills to survive in this tough world. I am their teacher, as well as their mother, friend, social worker and confidant. I can truly say teaching is my passion.

What my kids learn about innovation and entrepreneurship

They learn to explore their creative side and to step outside the box. They realize they don't have to be stuck in the continuous cycle of poverty that they life in. They can be successful, make the big bucks, and live a nice, comfortable lifestyle as long as they put the hard work in. They learn what it takes to create and develop a product. They learn and understand that they have the freedom to own their own business and that if they see a problem, they can create a business opportunity.

How I teach them to be motivated to succeed

I use hands-on activities, guest speakers and visuals. I discuss the struggles that I, as a single parent who has a master's degree, face every day due to the recent economy. I tell them that no matter what their disability is, they can overcome anything and be successful at what they choose – they just have to put forth the effort.

My secret approach to unleashing students' creativity

BE REALISTIC!!! Don't sugar-coat anything. My students come from diverse backgrounds. It's no secret. Tap into their creative side. I have students who speak Spanish and English. They have a skill others don't. Some of my students are talented artists – one would never know since they doodle in class. I ask over and over until my students finally cave and tell me what they enjoy and what makes them happy.

What I do to teach self-confidence

If you lack self-confidence, you will not be able to sell a product or service. One must have that to succeed in life in general. I teach it for them personally and as a tool to succeed as an entrepreneur.

My students' most important leadership skills

Their ability to "hustle." Many have to survive due to their home life. Their desire to want more in life is evident in the products and services they design in class, as well as their attendance in school on a daily basis. They are motivated, headstrong and driven.

The best way for them to learn those skills

Apply them every day. Encourage them to do their best. Never give up on them, even on their worst day. Encourage them to talk to other entrepreneurs who come from diverse backgrounds.

The most important thing teaching has taught me

No matter what, every student needs you. It is your responsibility to teach them; you owe them an education.

How has YEScarolina helped you develop your ability to teach entrepreneurial skills?

YEScarolina has been one of the most amazing accomplishments I have completed in addition to my certification to become a teacher. I always look for more ways to teach my students real-life skills, and YEScarolina's program and vision assisted me in becoming knowledgeable and qualified to teach entrepreneurship. Hats off to Mr. Bailey and the entire staff of YEScarolina for offering a program that meets the needs of all students and for providing educators the opportunity to teach entrepreneurship.

Debbie Jennings

Charleston Charter School for
Math and Science, Charleston
11th grade

"Whatever their interests are, there is a road to follow. All they need to do is ask the right questions and then follow that road."

Debbie Jennings understands what Socrates knew about effective teaching – the power of questions. She asks plenty of them, and when her students discover they can come up with the answers, their confidence and accomplishments grow. Jennings, who has been teaching eight years, lives in Charleston.

Why I teach

I teach because the youth are our future. To see the proverbial light bulb go off is a life-changing moment for the student and the teacher. It is an incredible process to witness.

What my kids learn about innovation and entrepreneurship

My kids learn that their imagination is unlimited – whatever they envision is a possibility. They just need to be willing to do the work to take their work to fruition.

How I teach them to be motivated to succeed

I expose my kids to the plethora of avenues that are available to them. Whatever their interests are, there is a road to follow. All they need to do is ask the right questions and then follow that road.

My secret approach to unleashing students' creativity

I believe in the Socratic method of teaching. I challenge them by asking question upon question. When they realize that they have the answers to these questions, they become confident and assertive. By being able to answer these questions, they believe in themselves.

What I do to teach self-confidence

I relate self-confidence to their creativity. I make them believe in themselves and make them realize that their ideas are viable and doable if that is what they really want.

My students' most important leadership skills

The most important leadership skill that my kids possess is self-confidence. If they believe in themselves, then there is no stopping them. They need to know that they have what it takes to become the person/leader that they want to be. By doing the work of having a strong business plan, they have the resource/information that they need to help them through the trying times of being an entrepreneur.

The best way for them to learn those skills

My students can realize their potential by getting to know themselves and by believing in themselves. You are only as strong as your weakest link. I encourage my students to seek the help that they need and to become more proficient in areas where they may need encouragement.

The most important thing teaching has taught me

Teaching entrepreneurship has taught me that each and every one of my students has the potential to be a success. Their success may not be what I think the definition of success is, but if they can define their own success and achieve it, then they have taught me more than I could possibly want.

How has YEScarolina helped you develop your ability to teach entrepreneurial skills?

YEScarolina has been a tremendous asset and resource for teaching entrepreneurship. Whatever a teacher needs to facilitate the entrepreneurship instruction in the classroom, YEScarolina can and does supply that information.

Any additional comments?

YEScarolina is one of the best avenues for youth in South Carolina that is available. YEScarolina gives our youth the instruction that is needed to help them become entrepreneurs and productive citizens.

Robin Keyes

Center for Accelerated Preparation, Columbia
7th-9th grades

"My goal is to encourage my students to dream."

Everyone harbors creativity, and Robin Keyes finds that guest speakers drive that point home. One, a poet and artist, helped the class design cards – which Keyes sends to her students. The lesson: Artists can be entrepreneurs. It's all about creativity. Keyes, who has taught entrepreneurship four years, lives in Columbia.

Why I teach

Teaching children is the best way to open your mind to the needs of others. I feel that I am the student, learning from them, and I have been surprisingly and greatly impacted by this opportunity. It is not easy, but I can say that teaching is the most memorable and rewarding experience.

What my students learn about innovation and entrepreneurship

Entrepreneurship is about dreaming and not putting limits on your dreams. Everyone has the potential to be creative, and it can be developed. My students learn that entrepreneurs started with a dream and that those dreams can become reality. My goal is to encourage my students to dream.

What I do to teach self-confidence

Confidence is a feeling that cannot be taught; it is something that is achieved by an experience. Many children go unnoticed and feel that nobody believes in them. When they believe that they are heard and understood, than they will experience self-confidence. Encouraging them to go for it and letting them know that someone believes that they can accomplish something is the best way to develop confidence.

The most important thing teaching has taught me

Teaching has taught me that all children are amazing and everyone deserves to feel the possibility of their dreams becoming a reality.

How has YEScarolina helped you develop your ability to teach entrepreneurial skills?

This is my third year teaching the YEScarolina program, and I began this process just like a new student – unsure, nervous and scared of failing. This program has made me a better person and opened my mind to the possibilities of these children. They all have amazing potential that I did not initially recognize. YEScarolina has helped me develop my ability to be a better teacher by having an open mind while creating an environment that reinforces the value of creative thinking.

Any special stories you'd like to share?

My favorite lessons always involve hands-on activities for the children. We had a guest speaker who is a poet, author and artist who designs note cards and greeting cards. He helped our children with the process of designing their own cards. One class designed a school signature card, and one class designed a holiday card. We chose one card from each class to be recognized. I printed our holiday cards and sent them to the students' families. I also printed the school cards and use them regularly for thank-you cards.

This experience exposed the children to meeting someone who is an entrepreneur, and the activity tied in nicely with inventions and creativity lessons from the NFTE program. The children learned that an entrepreneur can be an artist, and our activity reinforced the value of creative thinking. Everyone has the potential to be creative, and we all realized that we have this potential due to the time spent with our guest. We all developed our creativity and learned that YES YOU CAN develop a product!

Anne H. Marcengill

Greenville Senior High Academy, Greenville
9th-12th grades

"Students love to talk. Talking is sharing. If we listen, really listen, to what others are saying, we learn."

If young people are to believe in themselves, says Anne H. Marcengill, they must know that someone else believes in them – that they have something valuable to offer, that their dreams are worthy of pursuit. Marcengill has been teaching 14 years and lives in Simpsonville.

Why I teach

There is nothing more exciting than being a part of a young person's world. Teaching is an avenue for me to do just that. As in anything we do in life, being in a young teen's world is up one minute and down the next. However, when that light bulb goes on and I catch a glimpse – I've lived! Many times there is no visible light bulb, and that's when I hope and pray that one day something we've studied – a concept, a vocabulary word, an equation, a formula – helps my student make a wise and thoughtful decision for his life.

What my kids learn about innovation and entrepreneurship

Hopefully, they learn that innovation and entrepreneurship are one in the same. We all need entrepreneurial skills for whatever we do in life. Whether we own our own businesses or work for someone else, we need to be innovative and entrepreneurial. We are always in the business of "innovatively 'packaging' ourselves."

How I teach them to be motivated to succeed

We look at the skills and characteristics of entrepreneurs; we study the concepts an entrepreneur uses to build his or her business; we decide on a business we could start; we make a business plan; and we apply all of this to ourselves and what we want. Hopefully, we are all learning to decide what we want and how to go after it.

My secret approach to unleashing students' creativity

It's no secret. I believe you must believe in each student – believe that each one has something to offer and is capable of capturing his or her dreams – and each student must know that you genuinely do believe in him.

What I do to teach self-confidence

Example–I try to show self-confidence in my decisions, my subject matter, my life experiences. As a class, we talk about how we start, where we want to finish, and how to get there. We write a business plan. Some may never own their own business, but they understand how to start at the beginning and work with what they have.

Sharing–My story, someone else's story, their own stories help students understand that we all struggle, though some have it easier than others. We study other entrepreneurs, we listen to guest speakers, we work with the concept that life is what we, ourselves, make of it.

Talking–Students love to talk. Talking is sharing. If we listen, really listen, to what others are saying, we learn.

Admittance–Teens/students need to know that I know I don't know everything, and its okay to admit to that. If at all possible, I involve them in helping me to learn, helping me to find a way to learn something new.

My students' most important leadership skills

The ability to express themselves and their beliefs; communicating.

The best way for them to learn those skills

Practice at communication with their peers, with teachers, with other adults. We do a lot of presenting in class. Students make projects as a group, by themselves, and they present to their peers. That is one of the hardest things a non-speaker must do – present to his peers. At times, each student must convince his group, the class, and me to believe in what they believe in (at least enough to buy, endorse and promote the product or service). We practice communication daily whether it is in talking or presenting to a group. If you cannot communicate, you lose your chance at success.

The most important thing teaching has taught me

I've learned that we continue to learn no matter how much school we've had, how many years we've done something, how much we think we know. Children of all ages (elementary and beyond) have so much to share. I must listen; I must respond to what I hear. I must give chances for self-expression. I must encourage creativity. I must believe that every child has something to offer. I must help them learn how to use themselves to their best advantage. I've learned that more than teaching facts, teachers need to teach how to explore and how to continue to find the best in ourselves.

How has YEScarolina helped you develop your ability to teach entrepreneurial skills?

I had never taken an entrepreneurship course when I took the course from YEScarolina. Jimmy Bailey's excitement is hard not to catch. I have used every project they used in teaching us; I've used the plans and hints that others in the class (and other classes) have shared. The support from YEScarolina is phenomenal, and I know that YEScarolina is behind the students and teachers, all over South Carolina, a hundred percent!

Any special stories you'd like to share?

My entrepreneurship class is at the end of the day; over 50 percent of the students did not sign up to take the class. We struggled. Nothing seemed to interest them; no project was taken seriously. Slowly students began catching on. This, if nothing else, could be an easy A, they thought. One student continued to resist. Here and there when he did listen, he sometimes commented with depth, but he always added something funny or ridiculously silly. We listened, though, and soon the class learned he was involved in a business designing T-shirts. He makes no money, but he's involved. As our lessons progressed (a lemonade stand project, the Hershey bar packaging project, the prototype of a product project), he began sharing bits and pieces of his dreams. He has an in-depth desire to own his own business. Parts of our curriculum on "How to Start a Small Business" – the projects, the making of a business card with a logo, and beginning a business plan – have inspired him to talk seriously about his dreams. In his own way, this student is very innovative. I believe the exposure in this class, using YEScarolina's approach to entrepreneurship, will one day be invaluable to this young man.

Our school has a coffee shop run by the Career and Technology Department. This has been an invaluable tool for teaching costs vs. sales; how to manage a business; how an entrepreneur must be innovative; and how, no matter how good your product is, that often is not enough. Although we have no competition, we have had major dips in sales, almost no enthusiasm for the shop, and a resistance of students to work. Our entrepreneur students are actually experiencing what it is like for a business owner in the real world.

Any additional comments?

What I have learned from YEScarolina, and from my students, has been of extreme importance to me. I have reignited a spark of my own for the business world and renewed my enthusiasm for teaching others how to learn and experience success.

Jennifer Molnar

Rock Hill High School, Rock Hill
9th-12th grades, business education

"Treat every student with respect, and as if he or she has already achieved success. That type of encouragement can only help the student to become a success."

Peer influence plays a crucial role in molding students, and Jennifer Molnar understands the importance of keeping it positive. She showcases the success stories of young people and others who are following their dreams to greatness. Molnar lives in Rock Hill and has taught for five years.

Why I teach

I want to be a component of tomorrow's success and provide new and exciting opportunities for the students of today. Business knowledge is essential in life; it is in every aspect of our everyday lives. I believe if we teach students about business at a young age, they will realize their potential in life. In the world of business, the only limitation is the limit of believing in oneself, and with YEScarolina we teach students that the sky's the limit and everyone has the ability to be successful.

What my kids learn about innovation and entrepreneurship

They learn that entrepreneurship starts with an idea, and everyone has a great idea. With innovation, creativity, and perseverance, they can make their dreams a reality, at any age!

How I teach them to be motivated to succeed

I share success stories of other students who have achieved success with their business ideas. I teach high school students and have learned that peer influence can work in wonderful ways, especially when a teacher uses it to his or her advantage. I have a "Wall of Fame" in my room that showcases past and present student success stories. The success stories are not always from my classroom; rather, they come from a variety of sources such as other academic departments, sports teams, or organizations outside of the school. The important thing is for students to see other students achieving success and how these students are recognized for their commitment to greatness.

My secret approach to unleashing students' creativity

I believe in them unconditionally!

What I do to teach self-confidence

I become the student's No. 1 fan. It all goes back to customer service; treat students how you'd like to be treated as a student. Treat every student with respect, and as if he or she has already achieved success. That type of encouragement can only help the student to become a success.

My students' most important leadership skills

Supporting each other and evaluating each other's work to enable their fellow classmates to become better business entrepreneurs.

The best way for students to learn entrepreneurial skills

Provide them the opportunity for hands-on experience. Encourage all ideas, and never give up on a student. Become his or her biggest investor when it comes to support and self-confidence. When a teacher believes in a student's idea and is excited, it is amazing how much potential is unleashed within the student. Students want to work harder and give 110 percent effort because they know someone believes and supports their success.

The most important things teaching has taught me

The three most important principals teaching has taught me are patience, endurance and a commitment to excellence. I am a more patient person because even though I have a lesson plan, that doesn't mean the day will go according to the plan. The lesson plan doesn't ensure all the information will be absorbed by all students, and I need to go back and re-teach and re-plan, and that is okay. Teaching is a profession where you need endurance; you have to stay in the race until the objective is reached by all parties, and you cannot give up! I have a commitment to excellence because students need to know the norm is excellence. Once that has been established, they will rise to expectations.

How has YEScarolina helped you develop your ability to teach entrepreneurial skills?

I am confident that I would not be the teacher I am today without the support and education I received from YEScarolina. When I attended my first YEScarolina workshop in July 2008, I was new to the teaching field and wasn't sure what direction I would take as a teacher. When I completed the workshop, I knew I would a better teacher. YEScarolina provided me the tools to help students be successful in and outside the classroom. I attribute my success as a teacher to YEScarolina. YEScarolina celebrates not only greatness in students but also greatness in teaching, encouraging teachers to be the best they can be – for which I will forever be grateful!

Any additional comments?

Thank you, Jimmy Bailey, for making YEScarolina a reality and giving the priceless gift of entrepreneurship education to so many teachers across the state. I believe South Carolina will become the leader in entrepreneurial businesses because of YEScarolina. Even if the students are not completely aware of the opportunity they are given in the classroom, one day when they are on the cover of Forbes or Money magazine they will be thanking YEScarolina for giving them the fundamental education and capital to make their businesses a reality.

Deborah Niiya
Silver Bluff High School, Aiken

"Forgive mistakes, and give them room to try again."

On the road to success, students must explore: They need to understand how the world can use the talents each can share, says Deborah Niya, a teacher for 11 years who lives in Aiken. By helping others, students help themselves to develop a profitable career, with products and services they know will be in demand.

Why I teach

To develop work skills and life skills toward a stimulating, productive life.

What my kids learn about innovation and entrepreneurship

If they understand themselves and the world around them, they can identify many exciting ways to share their talents with the world. If they tap into their creativity, they can meet the needs of others, thereby investing in a rewarding pursuit of life toward a future of their dreams. Entrepreneurship is a great way to do this.

How I teach them to be motivated to succeed

We try to identify what they need and want from life and their future, and then we try to figure out how to get there.

My secret approach to unleashing students' creativity

Value their talents and encourage their exploration and development of them.

What I do to teach self-confidence

Forgive mistakes, and give the students room to try again.

vMy students' most important leadership skills

Support of others.

The best way for them to learn those skills

Experiential learning.

The most important thing teaching has taught me

It has taught me to explore a broader perspective of the world and how we shape each other. Sometimes the seemingly smallest act means everything to another.

How has YEScarolina helped you develop your ability to teach entrepreneurial skills?

The training and support provide the foundation to build educational experiences that build lives.

Roger Roberg
Beaufort High School, Beaufort
10th-12th grades

"Once students match their talents, interests, and sense of purpose, it can create unstoppable synergy."

Integrity matters most, says Roger Roberg, who has been teaching for seven years and lives in Beaufort. Other leadership skills depend upon one's fundamental honesty, principles and credibility. All students have creative potential, and those of good character are the ones likely to thrive. Often, he says, a teacher's job is to guide them – "and then get out of their way."

Why I teach

This generation is very important and will face many challenges. Each student must be fully prepared for the future in order to reach full potential. It is my job to be part of that forming process by meeting students where they currently are in their development and helping them to progress.

What my kids learn about innovation and entrepreneurship

I have a quote in my room from Einstein that basically says, "You can't solve today's problems with the same level of thinking as when you created them." In order to serve needs and solve problems, you have to step out of the box and take risks. Oprah Winfrey, Steve Jobs, Jerry Wang, Bill Gates, Russell Simmons, and Warren Buffet all are great examples to learn about in class to tie together concepts of innovation and entrepreneurship.

How I teach them to be motivated to succeed

All great entrepreneurs had lots of obstacles to overcome, and they learned to look at obstacles and failure the same way as great body-builders do: Training to failure is a good thing and the only way to grow. In addition, all people have the keys to success within them; they just have to find the right door. Once students match their talents, interests, and sense of purpose, it can create unstoppable synergy.

My secret approach to unleashing students' creativity

The secret is that students are naturally creative. Sometimes teachers just need to give them guidance on a topic and then get out of their way.

What I do to teach self-confidence

Self-confidence is best developed through previous successes. Students need to have "small victories" so that they can continue to build on that and create a pattern of success.

My students' most important leadership skills

It is hard to develop other leadership skills without the leadership skill of integrity. If you are not honest, forthright, and believable by other people, it is impossible to go any further in a leadership situation.

The best way for them to learn those skills

Give them opportunities to show you what they are made of.

The most important thing teaching has taught me

I think the Beatles had it right: "And in the end, the love you take is equal to the love you make." Teaching has reminded me of that.

How has YEScarolina helped you develop your ability to teach entrepreneurial skills?

YEScarolina has a great training program and support staff. Jimmy Bailey is one of the most positive people on the planet, and he gives 100 percent to helping these young people be successful. YEScarolina's outreach to teachers in South Carolina is truly inspiring.

Any special stories you'd like to share?

I am inspired by my students. One, in particular, is Hunter Dean. Hunter started a business called Beaufort Biofuels. Initially his idea was to help the environment, earn a couple of bucks, and have free fuel. Long story short: he was selected by YEScarolina and the Network for Teaching Entrepreneurship to represent South Carolina at the Oppenheimer Funds/NFTE Young Entrepreneur of the Year contest held in New York. Hunter made a brilliant showing at the competition and had a great business plan. Since then he has inspired countless others in entrepreneurship, alternative energy, and the environment through being featured in a book, television interviews and school seminars. A small idea that grows to inspire others through innovation and entrepreneurship – wow!

Any additional comments?

Being recognized by YEScarolina, whether you are a teacher or a student, is incredibly motivating.

Misty Rohaly

Wando High School, Mount Pleasant

10th-12th grades

"It is crucial for me to be in a good mood and have a good rapport with the students because some of them might not have that at home."

Students learn and gain confidence from one another, says Misty Rohaly, and as a teacher she makes the most of their innate desire to succeed. She shows them concepts and examples of how turning passions into profits is possible and strives to help students feel comfortable working with one another. She lives in Mount Pleasant and has been a Wando High teacher for five years.

Why I teach

I believe that all students have some talent or special characteristic that will make them productive members of society. In teaching entrepreneurship, I help them figure out what that is and then try to show them how to make a living doing what they like to do.

What my kids learn about innovation and entrepreneurship

If you don't take the risk, you'll never know how far you could go.

How I teach them to be motivated to succeed

It's very difficult to "teach" motivation. Motivation is a driving force that can be triggered by things such as interest in the actual task, or a reward of some sort. Therefore we study other entrepreneurs as examples and listen to many guest speakers who are willing to tell us their stories. The unique aspect of this class is that the students get to pick whatever it is that interests them and focus on it for most of the class; therefore, intrinsic motivation should already be in place. Once they realize that they can make money doing what they like, the extrinsic motivation kicks right in! All I do is show them a few concepts on how turning their passion into profits is possible.

My secret approach to unleashing students' creativity

It is really no secret. We play a lot of games such as "Trash to Treasure" and do a lot of problem-solving activities. We also do "Apprentice"-style tasks that make the students think laterally, and we have invention contests with prizes. I always have them present their projects to the rest of the class. That encourages them to be funny/creative, and it also gets them used to being in front of people presenting their ideas.

What I do to teach self-confidence

I try to make things relevant to real life. We talk about different products that are on the market that seem silly but also seem to be making money. Students are encouraged to talk about their ideas no matter how "silly" they might seem. In my opinion, students gain confidence from one another, so most of the hands-on activities are collaborative. Again, throughout the entire class, students are presenting information in different ways and making commercials and performing jingles, etc. Humor is encouraged, too! The key for me has been to make each student feel comfortable in this kind of setting.

My students' most important leadership skills

Being confident and being able to communicate ideas.

The best way for them to learn those skills

Collaboration, practice, and trial and error.

The most important thing teaching has taught me

You never know what kind of background or home life that these students have. I have 90 minutes or less every day to make a positive impact on so many teenagers. It is crucial for me to be in a good mood and have a good rapport with the students because some of them might not have that at home. Teaching has also taught me that most kids actually desire discipline and respect me for enforcing rules, something I didn't realize my first year.

How has YEScarolina helped you develop your ability to teach entrepreneurial skills?

It has done so in many ways. Mainly it has been the constant support. I had no idea that YEScarolina would offer so much support when I initially signed up to take the NFTE course. YEScarolina has allowed me to network with others who teach this most important concept all over the world. YEScarolina has also supplied great resources such as books and guest speakers.

Norma Jean Rockwell

Carver-Edisto Middle School, Cope
6th-8th grades

"I teach motivation to succeed by giving the students tangible products to sell for their own profits. Not only do these students earn a grade, they earn cash."

Not everyone learns the same way, and Norma Jean Rockwell recognizes the value of projects-based teaching, which "reaches more students than a single textbook." She makes sure each student group encompasses diverse skills among members so teammates learn from one another. Rockwell, who lives in Blackville, has been teaching for seven years.

Why I teach

I teach because I love sharing my knowledge with others and learning from my students.

What my kids learn about innovation and entrepreneurship

My kids learn how to create a profitable product and run their own small business. The 12-week entrepreneurship class is designed to create a delivery business of preordered cookies and candy baskets. The basic business plan is written throughout the course, culminating with a final project of a completed business plan.

How I teach them to be motivated to succeed

I teach motivation to succeed by giving the students tangible products to sell for their own profits. Not only do these students earn a grade, they earn cash in these 12 weeks.

My secret approach to unleashing students' creativity

I group the students based on a multiple intelligence survey. Each student completes the survey and is grouped with students with stronger skills in other elements. Each group is homogenous with a strong writer, artist, mathematician, organizer, and speaker. Each group competes with other groups for creativity, productivity and sales.

What I do to teach self-confidence

I teach self-confidence with encouragement for all. I don't tell the students how to run their business, but instead model and offer suggestions. The easiest method to teach self-confidence is to hand the students the cash they have earned.

My students' most important leadership skills

I think my students' most important leadership skill is the ability to communicate with each other.

The best way for them to learn those skills

Their ideas, needs, and demands are shared among the groups, which leads to sales of their products to classmates, teachers, and family members.

The most important thing teaching has taught me

Not everyone learns in the same manner. Project-based learning reaches more students than a single textbook.

**How has YEScarolina helped you develop your
ability to teach entrepreneurial skills?**

YEScarolina developed my ability to teach entrepreneurial skills with
more than a week of activities useful in the classroom of middle-
school and adult students. I had experience as an entrepreneur but
not as an entrepreneurship teacher. My approach to teaching entrepreneurship changes as my students change, but the one constant
is the ability of the students to create their own business and earn
money. Cash is the best motivator. It is fun to watch the groups
combine their ideas and skills into a profitable business. I, and they,
couldn't have succeeded without YEScarolina.

Eva Rutiri
West Ashley High School, West Ashley
9th-12th grades

"I have learned to love the spontaneity of teenagers. I love all the fresh ideas from a young person. "

Eva Rutiri's approach runs from the personal to the global. Students need to know that they and their ideas matter to someone – and to the community. Once they feel validated, a world of opportunities awaits them, and Rutiri emphasizes cultural diversity and e-commerce innovation. A teacher for 25 years, Rutiri lives in Charleston and was named the county district's teacher of the year for 2011.

Why I teach

I teach because of my passion to serve as a good role model to high school students and make a positive impact in a child's life. I love all business-related courses but have a knack for technology. Since I have this love for learning technology, I am also stretching and sharing new technological advances in my classroom. I am particularly inspired to teach high school students how to be global entrepreneurs and challenge them to implement their businesses online.

What my kids learn about innovation and entrepreneurship

My students learn the foundation of starting a business by exploring many successful American entrepreneurs. We also look at entrepreneurship on a global level and study the many successful online businesses to understand the world of e-commerce. Since I participated in an SC Global Entrepreneurship Exchange Program with Denmark, my students had the opportunity to exchange ideas with students in Denmark. It's great to see two different cultural perspectives, and this helps students understand entrepreneurship on a global level. Therefore, it inspires them to be innovative.

How I teach them to be motivated to succeed

I motivate each child by validating that he or she is important on a personal level. I challenge them to be creative thinkers and contribute to the community. My strategy for success in the classroom starts with implementing projects that are creative so they will "buy in." Once they have bought in, I encourage them to present and learn how to sell their ideas. All projects have peer evaluations, and winners are selected and recognized.

My secret approach to unleashing students' creativity

My secret approach is to showcase technology and set high expectation for all students to do their best job. I have found that utilizing technology inspires students because they like to be engaged and challenged on this level.

What I do to teach self-confidence

I teach self-confidence by having each student create a Career Portfolio. They create a hard copy and keep it in the classroom. The portfolio organizes all career assessments that profile a student's aptitude for a chosen career field. Once they recognize they have a talent for a certain career, I see them mature and take things a little more seriously. The results of the career assessment seem to give them an identity that validates their self-worth.

My students' most important leadership skills

The leadership skills in my students evolve as they define their self-worth by the following: participating in career-related classroom activities, creating innovative ideas with small-business projects, and exploring technological advances that help them to sell their innovations. Once these foundations are in place, students blossom and have the confidence to share their great ideas in the marketplace.

The best way for them to learn those skills

Students must learn these skills by watching a role model practice basic business relationships with the community, and that's me. As a teacher, it is important that I show up for class every day as a professional and very prepared. In order for a child to buy in to a program, you have to be on top of your game, structured, respectful, and show a great appreciation for diversity in the classroom.

The most important thing teaching has taught me

Teaching has taught me to be a better person. I have learned to be respectful, appreciate diversity, and be patient. I have learned to love the spontaneity of teenagers. I love all the fresh ideas from a young person. I have truly learned that their ideas are much better than mine.

How has YEScarolina helped you develop your ability to teach entrepreneurial skills?

YEScarolina has helped me to take a complicated topic of entrepreneurial business plans and break it down for the student. The PowerPoint template used to create a business plan is brilliant. It gives a teacher a step-by-step approach to teach a topic that can sometimes overwhelm the teacher and student. The textbook does a great job of teaching all entrepreneurial standards so the student can understand it on a basic, intermediate and advanced level.

Any special stories you'd like to share?

YEScarolina offers an opportunity for young people to take their innovations to another level. YEScarolina has the right connections to make an entrepreneurship student a celebrity if he or she has the right business idea. Most importantly, YEScarolina does an amazing job of recognizing outstanding entrepreneurship students across the state of South Carolina. The award banquet that is held in October is one of the most stunning events I have ever attended. YEScarolina does a stand-out job showcasing the best of young entrepreneurs in the great state of South Carolina.

Any additional comments?

Entrepreneurship is a great course that should be offered in every high school across America. I believe we are doing a child a disservice if we do not offer this course that will teach basic business ideas and couple it with web-page design. These are the jobs of the future.

Joyce Simons

Dent Middle School, Columbia

7th-8th grades

"YEScarolina offers a progressive course that could define the future for our state and country to compete in a global workforce, which is a challenge that we all face."

Before pursuing her passion for education, Joyce Simons owned a mortgage company – but got tired of getting people into debt. "I owe a debt to help people," she explained. A teacher for thirteen years, she lives in Columbia and is a native of that city.

Why I teach

I teach in hopes of making a difference for the future.

What my kids learn about innovation and entrepreneurship

In my class, my students learn problem-solving skills and how to apply these skills in their everyday lives. They recognize that such skills can make a difference in their school performance and community as future leaders.

How I teach them to be motivated to succeed

I use various types of motivational videos – such as one on micro-sculptor Willard Wigan and the art he creates in "The Eye of a Needle," and the music video "Man in the Mirror" by Michael Jackson – and competitive games that allow students to apply their skills to win prizes.

My secret approach to unleashing students' creativity

My secret approach to unleashing my students' creativity is making sure that the resources that they need (books, pencils, computer, posters, crayons, music, and space) are readily available and none is restricted so that they may create with freedom.

What I do to teach self-confidence

I approach each one of my students as an extended-family member. I have their best interest within my heart in hopes that they will develop strong character to become productive members in society.

My students' most important leadership skills

I think the most important leadership skill is the ability to use their natural skills to give back to their communities. I provide a venue for my students to actively engage in community service. In an after-school program, my entrepreneurship students volunteer their time serving the American Red Cross, Souper Bowl of Caring, and Special Olympics. A partnership with higher-learning institutions provides mentoring and service-learning activities for my students that help them develop their internal skills for external good.

The best way for them to learn those skills

The way that my students learn skills of self-confidence and leadership is through practice and application, over and over again.

The most important thing teaching has taught me

The most important thing that teaching has taught me is how dreaming does develop into problem-solving, critical thinking, and creative skills. Those are what help all of us design an education and career plan and set goals to become competitive members within this global society.

How has YEScarolina helped you develop your ability to teach entrepreneurial skills?

YEScarolina has been extraordinary in helping provide the necessary resources to assure successful entrepreneurship classes. YEScarolina has helped me with teaching entrepreneurial classes with phenomenal professional developments and administrative and financial support. YEScarolina is solving problem that don't exist now by investing in human capital – our youth, our future leaders.

Any special stories you'd like to share?

One of my students says that he loves this course. He says he is an entrepreneur and his odd job has now become a business. He can use his talents to benefit himself and the community by owning and operating a small business. He encourages other students to take this course so they can gain a formal business plan for a successful future.

Any additional comments?

A formal course in entrepreneurship helps students develop stronger characters and problem-solving, creative and critical-thinking skills for safer and productive communities. When students learn that they are an essential part of society, they begin to think differently and positively about their future. I think that we have a moral obligation as communities of educators, parents, businesses and civic organizations to assure that every student is given the opportunity to a formal education of entrepreneurship. YEScarolina offers a progressive course that could define the future for our state and country to compete in a global workforce by solving problems of the future with creative and responsible workers.

Paul Smith II

Newberry College

Sophomore to senior level, and youths grades 6-12

"Each class setting has moments of life-changing events.... A once-shy person is able to stand and deliver a business plan in front of complete strangers."

E ntrepreneurship isn't just a "buzzword," says Paul Smith II, who has been teaching for six years and lives in Columbia. As the state leader for Future Business Leaders of America, he imparts a crucial message to the youth who will take society's reins: Take heart in the examples of those who have never let failure defeat them, who have thrived through hard work and innovation. Never, says Smith, be stifled by "the nemesis of fear."

Why I teach

I am an entrepreneur first and foremost and passionate about imparting my knowledge, pitfalls and successes to students, which extends beyond the textbook. Not surprisingly, the proverbial "light" of self-confidence is turned on in these kids, and that energy extends to their other studies. My philosophy is to connect academic theory with practical application by clearly identifying that a business/entrepreneurship opportunity exists in sports, social media, science, technology, engineering and math.

What my students learn about innovation and entrepreneurship

That it is more than a buzzword. Rather, they learn to find within themselves the skills to create an opportunity rather than wait for one to appear. To that end, they are pressed to think outside of the "box." Secondly, they are instructed how to shop the competition in terms of industry size and long-term outlook, barriers to entry, levels of customer service, and pricing strategies. This is accomplished through a combination of cold-calling, market research and consumer surveys. Then, via the SWOT (strengths, weaknesses, opportunities, and threats) analysis, they determine if that idea is a viable opportunity.

How I teach them to be motivated to succeed

They are taught this quote by Marva Collins: "If you can't make a mistake, you can't make anything." This frees the mind and classroom from the nemesis of fear. In addition, they are provided with backgrounds and profiles of companies and individuals who succeeded after failing several times. For example, WD-40 failed forty times before developing that historic formula. In fact, the product is named Water Displacement 40 as a memorial to the number of mistakes it took to achieve greatness. This also applies to Formula 409.

My secret approach to unleashing students' creativity

I give them real-life examples of entrepreneurism that made it against the odds or those who failed their way to success. I also create a fun learning environment by incorporating team-building exercises, field trips, guest speakers, brain teasers, and daily prizes. All of these activities include elements of surprise and enigma and maintain the students' focus on the entrepreneurship curriculum.

What I do to teach self-confidence

I often show the "Ten9Eight" video to all of my students, which gives real-life examples of students who've had personal challenges but have triumphed to become world changers. I also believe it's important that students realize mistakes will be made in life but those are the stepping stones to success.

My students' most important leadership skills

Thinking outside of the norm. Aim to think differently.

The best way for them to learn those skills

To make any course of instruction, faculty lecture, Q&A, or critical-thinking exercise relevant to their daily lives, we must teach them from where we can reach them.

The most important thing teaching has taught me

Educators are world changers. As an educator, I can shape, mold, and prepare a student for the real world. I have the ability to show students how to think outside of the norm and create their own path of success.

Any special stories you'd like to share?

Frankly, each class setting has moments of life-changing events that transform these kids from the "rest" into an entrepreneurial mindset that taps into their creativity and desires. Then, a once-shy person is able to stand and deliver a business plan in front of complete strangers. Moreover, students now have a greater respect and appreciation for the topics of math, science, English, and reading because they can apply these concepts to their businesses.

Any additional comments?

Jimmy Bailey is "The Order of the Palmetto" in my opinion for what he has done through our most prized natural resource, our kids. Through his unselfish efforts, YEScarolina has trained over 500 teachers across this great state (free of charge) which has translated into countless thousands of kids being outfitted with an entrepreneurial mindset and modus operandi that is the most important skill set in the global society of the twenty-first century.

Jean Vess

Strom Thurmond Career Center, Johnston
9th-12th grades

"Students learn how much we depend on one other in business; thus, how important networking is to building a thriving and lasting business."

Jean Vess says a big part of her job is to help each student choose a business to pursue. Passion, however, must lead to profit if a business is to survive and reach out to the community. That's why Vess, a teacher for 14 years who lives in Gilbert, encourages students to keep up with issues of the day and the global market.

Why I teach

I elected to teach business-education subjects to high school students because I knew that I would be able to share many experiences of the business world, as an employee in a large corporation as well as an entrepreneurial owner of a small business. With today's economy, I realize that success in their own business may be the only way for many students to develop wealth. Most importantly, in high school, entrepreneurial activities help build good citizenship and self-confidence.

What my kids learn about innovation and entrepreneurship

The first thing they learn in my class is that all businesses must make a profit to succeed. I teach them that businesses also do many wonderful things for their community, but to establish a viable business they must first succeed in making a profit. My students explore countless ways that they can develop a business using their individual expertise, education, skills, and hobbies. In class, students learn how much we must depend on one another in business; thus, how important networking is to building a thriving and lasting business. I teach each student that operating a small business during high school and college will help them with needed tuition and will give them experience in the business world. In fact, I stress that operating their own business in high school offers them just as much experience, and maybe more, as completing an internship.

How I teach them to be motivated to succeed

I relate all of the stories of competition and success from NFTE, YEScarolina, and former students to build motivation and excitement, and to prove to each student that he or she can be successful in business. Seeing that others have succeeded at Strom Thurmond Career Center helps each student to develop enthusiasm about our plans. Relating the experiences of my past students who have participated in YEScarolina, SIFE, and NFTE competitions is a real motivator. Each student in my entrepreneurship and marketing classes is required to develop a complete business plan that is applicable to high-school level of experience and to the skills already developed. My big job is to help each student search within to decide what type of business to develop. I always try to find people who have succeeded in similar businesses to help them believe in their abilities, and in the power of capitalism.

My secret approach to unleashing students' creativity

I give them the tools from the textbook, and then encourage brainstorming to decide on the business that will best suit their individual interests, qualifications and experiences. Sharing some of these skills and experiences in class helps most students to gain confidence in what they have already accomplished. This confidence helps build momentum for success in business, as well as school. Since technology is a growing part of all business processes, I teach them about the use of social networking sites to network and to sell. Since I have also begun to teach a web-design class this year, I am able to incorporate ideas about the Internet for their business plans and to encourage them to take the web-page class later on to further expand their skills for business.

What I do to teach self-confidence

I share my personal business experiences with students. Since my family has operated a small business, and I worked for many years for a large corporation, I know that I have many real-world experiences to relate to them about success in business. I teach them that just knowing and expecting what will happen in a business is good preparation. It also gives a person a chance to prepare backup plans, and always plan for re-evaluating after trying new ideas. I definitely teach them that having well-thought-out plans will make them a success in any endeavor in life.

My students' most important leadership skills

Good team leadership skills will serve them well as a business owner, or as an employee. They also learn how to network with businesses to expand their knowledge about business, and to help them to find mentors and investors. As students work on our class social entrepreneurship plan each year, they must use networking skills to collaborate with business leaders, as well as work with teachers and leaders in our career center and school to complete the business plan successfully. As students work on their own individual business plan, they most definitely must be the leader of all activities within the plan.

The best way for them to learn those skills

I require all students each year not only to work on their individual business plan, but also to work in a team to develop a social entrepreneurship business plan, and actually to carry out the work in the plan. With the help of a small local grant, this year the students are working in collaboration with our reading initiative team in Edgefield County. They are writing stories with lots of pictures, as well as good morals for kindergarten-age children – a project that has led to many discussions on ethics. They will publish these stories in a book for all of the kindergarten classes in the district. So many of the young children in our district come from homes where there are no books, and no emphasis on the importance, as well as the fun, of reading. Since my students are not allowed to sell a product or service at school, the class works as a team on this project to develop the entire business plan, learn to budget to stretch the funds we have, and learn the importance of doing something for others.

The most important thing teaching has taught me

Teaching has taught me that you never make assumptions about students. Sometimes the student whom you first perceive as unwilling to learn new skills is the very student who excels.

How has YEScarolina helped you develop your ability to teach entrepreneurial skills?

YEScarolina has been my guiding light in developing new ways to interest my students in this class. The books and workbooks provided have given each student an effective way to understand how business operates. Just the one page that deals with "The Economics of One Unit" offers immeasurable information that our textbook did not give. To me, this is the key to understanding what works and what doesn't in a planned business. My lectures emphasize the use of this knowledge to be as sure as one can be that a business will pay a profit before starting the operation. I use teaching moments to discuss the economy. I want my students to be able to think for themselves, and learn how to investigate on their own the changes and laws that local and national government make that will affect their ability to succeed in their business. I really want them to become interested in keeping up with the issues of the day and making good personal decisions about their future. I stress to them that education about business and finances is the key to being prepared for what is happening in the global market, both today and in the future.

Any special stories you'd like to share?

My experience last year with our social entrepreneurship plan for the Youth Entrepreneurial Action Services was a success. This success was based on lots of hard work by the students, and the information they used from the NFTE Business Plan PowerPoint to help develop the plan. The plan included our showing appreciation to all teachers in the Strom Thurmond Career Center. The students had $100 to spend, with 20 teachers. They made photographs of teaching moments, and a motivational PowerPoint Presentation about all of the teachers to present to each teacher on CD. They also made gifts for a gift basket for each teacher. This provided lots of creative moments, as well as networking with community leaders and our horticulture department to help with some of the gifts. The whole process was successful, especially with all students getting involved.

Any additional comments?

I would like to express my appreciation for all of the inspiration and information afforded to me by YEScarolina. This keeps me going, when the going gets tough. This year I am teaching a new Dreamweaver Web Page Design class, as well as entrepreneurship, and marketing. We are able to tie many of the activities into group projects. Since the web-page class is new, and I only received two days of training, it is a real challenge but one that I am really enjoying because I am able to bring all of the factors of marketing and business to these students. Also, all of these classes have been extended to a full year, and this gives more time, especially for the entrepreneur class to develop workable business plans.

Maria D'Angelo Williams
Fort Dorchester High School, North Charleston
9th-12th grades

"Always be positive. Some students live in poverty, abuse, neglect, and negativity. It is up to us as educators to give students a welcoming, safe, comfortable, and positive learning environment so that they can flourish."

Business success requires working cooperatively, networking, reaching out – and Maria D'Angelo Williams knows that developing those skills is a good place for her students to start. They need to get comfortable talking in front of others and supporting their views – and she gives them plenty of practice. She lives in Summerville and has been teaching for 11 years.

Why I teach

I love to work with high school students. They all have so much potential – many just do not know it yet and it has to be filtered out. They are like a piece of clay that just needs some attention to be molded, shaped, and evolved into a masterpiece! I know they can do things even when they think they can't. Many just need a little push, but some need a shove.

What my kids learn about innovation and entrepreneurship

They learn that they all have great ideas! They just need to turn that idea into a consumer need and opportunity by improving it or making it better. For an improvement to take place, it is necessary for people to change the way they make decisions, or make choices outside of their norm. So, I ask them to literally "think outside of the box." They do not necessarily need to have a new idea but improve on an already existing idea and sell it at a profit.

How I teach them to be motivated to succeed

I list positive entrepreneurial characteristics that students have given me, and then I list negative entrepreneurial characteristics that students have given me. I ask them where they rank on this list of positive/negative entrepreneurial characteristics. Then, I ask them where they want to be and what they need to do to get there. They create a plan at the beginning of the year to work on it throughout the school year. We then revisit this plan quarterly to measure their progress. If they are not making progress, we work on why, so they can meet this goal by the end of the year.

My secret approach to unleashing students' creativity

Most students are unbelievably creative. I have found that cooperative learning environments tend to allow students' creativity to come out. Sometimes, they feel more comfortable in a small group. After acceptance in that small group, then they feel more comfortable in a large group to unleash that creativity. A few activities that really unleash students' creativity have been the Pizza Pizzaz Activity, Redesigning the Hershey Bar Wrapper, and the Invention Contest. In addition, I have students create commercials for their businesses in groups. This activity has allowed me to see unbelievable creativity in creating a rap, poem, or jingle, adding music, artistic drawings, and outstanding commercials in PowerPoint, MovieMaker, Adobe PhotoShop, and on video.

My students' most important leadership skills

To feel comfortable talking and expressing their opinions and ideas in front of others and getting their points across using facts and information to support their points. Experience in interacting professionally with other students in a cooperative learning environment is essential to building their leadership skills. As they interact with others in a group environment, their leadership skills evolve. In addition, they need the experience of interacting with an audience as a presenter of information. As the researchers and creators of the presentations, they are the experts in their presentations. The more they practice interacting as a group and a presenter, the more their self-confidence and self-esteem increase and their leadership skills increase.

The best way for them to learn those skills

Being a professional in front of students and giving them a comfortable, safe learning environment allows students the opportunity to unleash their creativity and build self-confidence.

The most important thing teaching has taught me

To always be patient with all students, set a professional example, and always be positive. Students are always watching us. How we conduct ourselves in our interactions with adults and students is extremely important in teaching students how to do this successfully. In addition, as a teacher of extremely diverse student backgrounds, it is very important to be compassionate and understanding with students. We do not know what type of home life they have. Some students live in poverty, abuse, neglect, negativity, etc. Sometimes, school offers their only positive interactions. It is up to us as educators to give students a welcoming, safe, comfortable, and positive learning environment so they can flourish.

How has YEScarolina helped you develop your ability to teach entrepreneurial skills?

YEScarolina has most definitely allowed me to develop the ability to teach entrepreneurial skills through the outstanding training program and continuing education in entrepreneurship. The books supplied by NFTE are written in a very user-friendly format. The chapters are short and not overwhelming for the students. The hands-on review work, activities, case studies, and creation of the business plan allow rigor, relevance, and reinforcement of entrepreneurial skills taught in the book. So, by my teaching an understandable and simplified curriculum to the students, I have been able to become an expert in the entrepreneurial field. In addition, it gave my husband and me the much-needed push to start our own business. We presently own and operate Williams Rentals, which includes the ownership of an apartment complex and several homes as rentals in the North Charleston area. In addition, YEScarolina provided me the highlight of my teaching career when I received the YEScarolina Teacher of the Year in 2006 and the opportunity to attend the NFTE Advanced Teacher Forum in June of 2006 at Columbia University in New York. Also, one of my students received the YEScarolina Student of the Year and won a laptop. That same year, he earned over $16,000 in net profit. With YEScarolina's support, I have been able to teach entrepreneurial skills over the past six years to 336 students. Students entering the world of work and/or college have such an abundance of knowledge to help them succeed in business and life with support from this outstanding program.

Any special stories you'd like to share?

One year, one of my students created a unique on-line greeting card business where she actually created the greeting in the card (and specialized to receiver) and used her artistic abilities to create the front of the card. YEScarolina provided two business people from the community to meet with the student and me twice per month for advice in preparing for the NFTE Business Plan Competition. YEScarolina additionally flew this student and her father to New York and provided meals and accommodations. Without YEScarolina, this particular student would not have had such an enormous opportunity and wonderful experience during her senior year of high school. Even though she did not place in the "Top Ten" in the nation, she would not have had this opportunity without YEScarolina. I am so grateful to Jimmy Bailey and YEScarolina for providing the educational and financial support for students to travel and compete and add such amazing experiences to their learning.

LaQuinta S. Yates

Summerville High School, Summerville

9th-12th grades

"Every single child has a diamond within. As an educator, it is my job to help students make that diamond shine with true brilliance."

When a student approaches LaQuinta S. Yates with an idea for an entrepreneurial pursuit, she responds consistently with enthusiasm and compliments. Then comes her questioning – and she helps the student "turn this OK idea into a super idea." The Summerville resident has been teaching for 12 years.

Why I teach

I truly believe that today's children are tomorrow's leaders and it is my duty as an educator to educate them so that they are prepared for this task. I love working with high school students because they are creative and challenging.

What my kids learn about innovation and entrepreneurship

I have taught entrepreneurship for four years, and the one connection that I feel I have made with all my students is teaching them that creativity is one of the key components to becoming a successful entrepreneur. Creativity leads to innovative ideas.

How I teach them to be motivated to succeed

Motivation can be different for each student. I think one of the best ways is to show students examples of successful entrepreneurs who are around their age. I find articles (many from YEScarolina) about local students being successful as entrepreneurs, and I post these around the room. I think my students can relate because here is a student doing the same thing that they are trying to achieve. I also praise students when good grades are achieved, and I pair students together in groups to work on different activities so that they can motivate each other.

My secret approach to unleashing students' creativity

My approach is to always be enthusiastic about their ideas and compliment them on their ideas. I think this makes them feel more confident. I then try to ask questions to make them think more about their ideas so that they can see it from a different point of view and turn this OK idea to a super idea.

What I do to teach self-confidence

On the first day of school, I have students stand in front of the class to state their name and what do they hope to learn from entrepreneurship. From this day forth, it never stops. At least once a week, students stand in front of the class and do presentations. I hope that I am building their confidence through this exercise. At the end of the year, students present their business plans, and when I compare their presentations on the first day vs. their presentation on the last day of class, it is amazing how much they have grown and changed.

My students' most important leadership skills

Adaptability, confidence, competitiveness, drive, organization, persuasiveness, discipline, perseverance, risk-taking, and to have a vision. All leaders need these qualities in order to be successful.

The best way for them to learn those skills

Two of the best ways for students to learn these skills is through practiced class activities and teacher modeling. Although you may think a student is not paying attention, he or she is listening to some degree. If you are displaying these characteristics, they have an opportunity to see these characteristics firsthand, which is setting an example for them to follow.

The most important thing teaching has taught me

I think the most important lesson I have learned about being an educator is that every single child has a diamond within. As an educator it is my job to help students make that diamond shine with true brilliance.

How has YEScarolina helped you develop your ability to teach entrepreneurial skills?

YEScarolina has definitely helped me with teaching entrepreneurship. When I was first asked to teach entrepreneurship at my school, I was a little hesitant. I was not an entrepreneur, and I wasn't sure if I had the experience to teach the class. YEScarolina has been a support system that I can call on at anytime and get assistance. They have done many things to support me such as offering enrichment seminars, offering guest speakers, presenting reading materials, buying textbooks and workbooks for my students, and offering summer camps for my students. YEScarolina has truly been an excellent resource for assisting me with teaching entrepreneurship.

Any special stories you'd like to share?

The classes that YEScarolina offered to become a certified NFTE teacher were excellent. It gave me a strong foundation to begin teaching entrepreneurship. The chapter activities and lesson plans were very useful!

Any additional comments?

I would like to thank YEScarolina for all they have done to assist me in teaching entrepreneurship over the last four years. I look forward to continuing our relationship in the future.

Brianna Zhang

Francis Marion University YEScarolina outreach teacher
Middle school, high school and adults

*"Students learn to be open to innovation
and not set limits on what is possible."*

An entrepreneur is on the way to success when he or she recognizes that everyone has strengths and weaknesses, says Brianna Zhang of Florence, who has been teaching for four years. Identifying one's own true strengths is essential, she says, but it's also important to evaluate weaknesses – and see them as an opportunity for growth.

Why I teach

The ability to reach at least one student is the reason I want and continue to teach. I see my role as a bridge to understanding of entrepreneurship for the students. Entrepreneurship education has very challenging sections, but I love finding new and different ways to make the information clear and not intimidating.

What my students learn about innovation and entrepreneurship

My students are told that entrepreneurship is an opportunity that can be available to everyone. However, the opportunity is only accessible through the ability to work hard, openness to learning, and the strength to accept success and failure.

Students learn to be open to innovation and not set limits on what is possible. Providing the students with tools to think and be open-minded about innovation will help them continuously throughout their lives.

How I teach them to be motivated to succeed

In order to teach students about success, the students must first believe in their potential. It is my job to show them their potential through various class exercises, individual conferences, and class discussions. Most importantly, I let them know up front that just enough is not good enough and that success is not guaranteed but can only be obtained through anticipated preparation for a potential opportunity.

My secret approach to unleashing students' creativity

Unleashing students' creativity is really nothing more than providing the space to let them think and speak without fear of their idea being rejected. My classroom is a no idea kill zone. The idea may not have market potential but can provide a gateway to other ideas. Creativity is a critical part of the entrepreneurship curriculum and in life.

What I do to teach self-confidence

Self-confidence can be taught through expressing that all students have something to offer. The most important factor for an entrepreneur is the ability to fully evaluate one's strengths and weaknesses. Self-confidence is built when students understand their true strengths and can see their weaknesses as opportunity for growth.

My students' most important leadership skills

My students have a variety of leadership skills such as good communication, problem solving, and networking.

The best way for them to learn those skills

Leadership skills are best developed in a team atmosphere. This method requires students to exchange ideas in order to develop solutions while keeping the team on task. While one student may take the role of the leader, each member of the team will offer different aspects of what makes a good leader and therefore they will learn from each other.

The most important thing teaching has taught me

Teaching has taught me that the student is as much responsible for the learning process as the teacher. Teaching is a two-way street that allows new ideas, concepts, etc., to flow between the teacher and student. I am always eager to allow students to talk and share their experiences because I learn from them. I also have learned that the most effective teaching is conducted with loose structure. This means one must have an idea of what needs to be covered but be flexible to the shifts that may occur during discussions.

How has YEScarolina helped you develop your ability to teach entrepreneurial skills?

YEScarolina has ignited my passion for teaching entrepreneurship. Over the years, YEScarolina has provided continued support and training opportunities for all certified teachers. Furthermore, YEScarolina has gone above and beyond in recognizing and rewarding the teachers who further the YEScarolina mission. I am truly honored to partner with an organization that is setting the standard for entrepreneurship education. I am certainly looking forward to many years to come from YEScarolina.

Any special stories you'd like to share?

Jimmy Bailey is truly an exceptional and remarkable person. As a successful entrepreneur, he could simply just enjoy the life he has worked so hard to build for himself. Instead, he decided to take his experience and passion to change the life of not only the students of South Carolina but also of the teachers who have been trained. I have partnered with YEScarolina for over five years now, and I'm constantly in awe of the impact it has made in South Carolina. YEScarolina is a visionary organization with a profound mission.

YEScarolina Board of Directors

Youth Entrepreneurship South Carolina, YEScarolina, is the only organization in the state of South Carolina dedicated to teaching youth the principles of entrepreneurship and free enterprise. Recognizing that South Carolina's future is dependent upon a vibrant Entrepreneurial Economy, YEScarolina is preparing today's youth to be tomorrow's business owners and business leaders.

YEScarolina has helped thousands of young people from communities statewide build business skills and unlock their entrepreneurial creativity. To date, YEScarolina trained and certified over 500 South Carolina teachers on the subject of entrepreneurship. These educators in turn have touched and inspired thousands of young South Carolinians with a thirst for entrepreneurship. YEScarolina now offers entrepreneurship training to public school teachers statewide without charge.

YEScarolina is a program partner of the Network For Teaching Entrepreneurship (NFTE).

YEScarolina is a 501(c) 3 non-profit. Proceeds from the sale of this book benefit YEScarolina. Your tax deductible donations can be sent to the address below. Your help is appreciated.

YEScarolina
PO Box 210
Charleston, SC 29402

www.yescarolina.com

How can you use this book?

MOTIVATE

EDUCATE

THANK

INSPIRE

PROMOTE

CONNECT

Why have a custom version of *Teachers Reaching Out?*

- Build personal bonds with customers, prospects, employees, donors, and key constituencies

- Develop a long-lasting reminder of your event, milestone, or celebration

- Provide a keepsake that inspires change in behavior and change in lives

- Deliver the ultimate "thank you" gift that remains on coffee tables and bookshelves

- Generate the "wow" factor

Books are thoughtful gifts that provide a genuine sentiment that other promotional items cannot express. They promote employee discussions and interaction, reinforce an event's meaning or location, and they make a lasting impression. Use your book to say "Thank You" and show people that you care.

Printed in the USA
CPSIA information can be obtained
at www.ICGtesting.com
JSHW012043140824
68134JS00033B/3227